To Moll......

W9-BFD-487 ....!

Best Wishes
on Your Graduation
and in All the Years Ahead

For Your Graduation

Thoughts About Meeting
a Marvelous Goal...
and Reaching Out for New Horizons

Edited by Douglas Pagels

Blue Mountain Press™
Boulder, Colorado

Library of Congress Control Number: 2003115207
ISBN: 0-88396-794-4

ACKNOWLEDGMENTS appear on page 64.

Certain trademarks are used under license.

BLUE MOUNTAIN PRESS is registered in U.S. Patent and Trademark Office.

Printed in the United States of America.
First Printing: 2004

 This book is printed on recycled paper.

This book is printed on fine quality, laid embossed, 80 lb. paper. This paper has been specially produced to be acid free (neutral pH) and contains no groundwood or unbleached pulp. It conforms with all the requirements of the American National Standards Institute, Inc., so as to ensure that this book will last and be enjoyed by future generations.

Blue Mountain Arts, Inc.

P.O. Box 4549, Boulder, Colorado 80306

Contents

For Graduation Day

This is a day to give you
all the most wonderful wishes
that can be wished — and all
the happiest congratulations
the heart can hold.

May this day be a reflection...
of all the recognition you deserve.
All the determination that
lights your path.
All the wisdom that
guides your steps.

And all the happiness and success
that will be wished for you
long after this day has passed.

You are wished the best of luck
        and lots of dreams come true!

— Douglas Pagels

The day you wished arrived at last.

— John Dryden

I want to be among the many who are congratulating you and wishing you the very best from now on. There is nothing else quite like graduation and the big step out into the world of reality and hard facts, with the challenge that is always waiting there.

— Alfred Stuart Myers

Come now and celebrate.

— Aristophanes

Success is feeling good about who you
are, appreciating where you've been,
celebrating your achievements, and
honoring the distance you've already come.

— Sarah Ban Breathnach

Hats off to the past;
sleeves up for the future.

— Anonymous

Look to this Day, for it is Life,
The very Life of Life.
In its brief course lie all the verities
And realities of your existence:
The bliss of growth, the glory of action,
The splendor of beauty;
For yesterday is but a dream,
And tomorrow is only a vision;
But today, well lived,
Makes every yesterday a dream of happiness
And every tomorrow a vision of hope.
Look well, therefore, to this day!

— "Salutation to the Dawn"

The graduate who worthily receives a diploma, which as its very meaning signifies, is a "letter of recommendation," should esteem the event as one of the proudest and happiest of life.

— W. W. Dodge

I know not
what the future holds,
but I know
who holds the future.

— Anonymous

So many worlds, so much to do...
such things to be.

— Alfred, Lord Tennyson

Whatever you can do,
or dream you can, begin it.
Boldness has genius,
power, and magic in it.

— Johann Wolfgang von Goethe

Graduation
Wishes for You

Happiness. Deep down within.
Serenity. With each sunrise.
Success. In each facet of your life.
Close and caring friends.
Love. That never ends.

Special memories. Of all the yesterdays.
A bright today. With much to
   be thankful for.
A path. That leads to beautiful tomorrows.

Dreams. That do their best to come true.
And appreciation. Of all the wonderful
   things about you.

— Douglas Pagels

Life is a path to be explored.

— Anonymous

Each man and each woman of you I lead
    upon a knoll,
My left hand hooking you round the waist,
My right hand pointing to landscapes of
    continents and the public road.
Not I, not any one else can travel that road
    for you,
You must travel it for yourself.

— Walt Whitman

Go as far as you can see, and when you get there,
you will see farther.

— Anonymous

Two roads diverged in a yellow wood,
And sorry I could not travel both
And be one traveler, long I stood
And looked down one as far as I could
To where it bent in the undergrowth;

Then took the other, as just as fair,
And having perhaps the better claim,
Because it was grassy and wanted wear;
Though as for that, the passing there
Had worn them really about the same,

And both that morning equally lay
In leaves no step had trodden black.
Oh, I kept the first for another day!
Yet knowing how way leads on to way,
I doubted if I should ever come back.

I shall be telling this with a sigh
Somewhere ages and ages hence:
Two roads diverged in a wood, and I —
I took the one less traveled by,
And that has made all the difference.

— Robert Frost

Tell yourself it's O.K. if you don't know where you are going at every moment of your life.... You don't have to know where you're going — as long as you're on your way.

— Dr. Wayne W. Dyer

You have brains in your head.
You have feet in your shoes.
You can steer yourself
any direction you choose.

— Dr. Seuss

Along the way you will stumble, and perhaps even fall; but that, too, is normal and to be expected. Get up, get back on your feet, chastened but wiser, and continue on down the road.... Think of me. I will be watching and smiling and cheering you on.

— Arthur Ashe

This Is a Time of Wonderful Possibilities

As you go through the days of your life, busy with all the responsibilities the world has placed upon you, remember to keep the truly special things in mind.

Keep things in perspective: work, play, learning, living. Have happiness as a part of your priorities! Be creative and aware and wonderfully alive. Work hard, but know that it's for a reason. The seasons of your life would love for you to be as involved in their everyday passages as you can possibly be. If you can accomplish that, if you can always remember where to find your smile, and if you can stay close to the people who are at the center of your life, you have already traveled a very long way on the road to success...

New journeys await you. Decisions lie ahead, wondering... what you will do; where you will go; how you will choose when the choices are yours.

Remember that good decisions come back to bless you, over and over again. Work for the ability to choose wisely, to prosper, to succeed. Listen with your heart as well as your head, to the glimmers of truth that provide advice and inspiration to the hours of your days. And let those truths take you to beautiful places.

Touch the sky, and in your reach, believe, achieve, and aspire.

I hope your tomorrows take you to the summit of your goals, and your joys take you even higher.

— Douglas Pagels

I can do anything. I can be anything. No one ever told me I couldn't. No one ever expressed this idea that I was limited to any one thing, and so I think in terms of what's possible, not impossible.

— Whoopi Goldberg

I'd like to do everything I can to avoid being an old person who says, "Why didn't I do that? Why didn't I take that chance?"

— Barbra Streisand

When I look to the future, I see more possibilities than limitations.

— Christopher Reeve

Have the daring to accept yourself as a bundle of possibilities and undertake the game of making the most of your best.

— Henry Emerson Fosdick

The greatest achievement of the human
spirit is to live up to one's opportunities
and make the most of one's resources.

— Vauvenargues

It's a funny thing about life;
if you refuse to accept
anything but the best,
you very often get it.

— Somerset Maugham

My Graduation Advice to You

Each day is a blank page in the diary of your life. And there is something special you need to remember in order to turn your life story into the treasure it deserves to be.

This is how it works...

Follow your dreams. Work hard. Be kind. This is all anyone could ever ask: Do what you can to make the door open on a day that is filled with inspiration in some special way.

Remember: Goodness will be rewarded. Smiles will pay you back. Have fun. Find strength. Be truthful. Have faith. Don't focus on anything you lack.

Realize that people are the treasures in life, and happiness is the real wealth. Have a diary that describes how you are doing your best, and...

The rest will take care of itself.

— Douglas Pagels

Imagine... Here you are, on the high peak of a mountain. You can choose to wing your way toward the clouds, or you can simply walk the usual, ordinary paths that lead to the valley below.

Which choice will you make —
the well-worn paths or rising above it all?

Beautiful things await you
    if you can reach the heights.

— George Sand

Dream lofty dreams, and as you dream, so shall you become.

— John Ruskin

We can do whatever we wish to do provided our wish is strong enough.

— Katherine Mansfield

No bird soars too high, if he soars with his own wings.

— William Blake

Indeed, everybody wants to be a wow,
but not everybody knows exactly how.

— Ogden Nash

There are a lot of exciting adventures out there
just waiting for you — go out and find them!
Choosing a college... Deciding on a career...
These passages of life can all evoke fear in us,
and they all carry with them an element of risk.
However, we cannot let our fears hold us back
from experiencing these joys.

— Joan Lunden

I think the ones who survive in life do it by
hammering at it one day at a time. You do what
you have to do to get through today, and that
puts you in the best place tomorrow.

— Oprah Winfrey

As You Graduate...
Don't Ever Stop
Dreaming Your Dreams

Don't ever try to understand everything —
some things will just never make sense.
Don't ever be reluctant
    to show your feelings —
    when you're happy, give in to it!
    When you're not, live with it.
Don't ever be afraid to try to
    make things better —
    you might be surprised at the results.
Don't ever take the weight of the world
    on your shoulders...

Don't ever feel threatened by the future —
    take life one day at a time.
Don't ever feel guilty about the past —
    what's done is done. Learn from any
    mistakes you might have made.
Don't ever feel that you are alone —
    there is always somebody there for you
    to reach out to.
Don't ever forget that you can achieve
    so many of the things you can imagine —
    imagine that! It's not as hard as it seems.
Don't ever stop loving,
    don't ever stop believing,
        don't ever stop dreaming your dreams.

— Douglas Pagels

As you keep growing and learning
striving and searching
it is very important
that you pursue your own interests
without anything holding you back
It will take time
to fully understand yourself
and to discover what you
want out of life
As you keep growing and learning
striving and searching
I know that the steps in your journey
will take you on the right path

— Susan Polis Schutz

What matters is that you can move on, you can grow...

— Kelsey Grammer

You've got a big heart. Keep it filled with happiness. You've got a fascinating mind. Keep finding new ways to grow. Keep yearning. Keep learning. Keep trying. Keep smiling. And keep remembering that so many wishes go with you... everywhere you go.

— Douglas Pagels

We were privileged to meet great teachers...
who pushed our horizon wider, gave us
greater openness of mind and a more
flexible way of thinking. They challenged us
to see the star and follow the gleam.

— Ethel Percy Andrus

It would be nice if we were each born with a
manual on how to live, or were taught how
to do so early in life by experts.

— Bernie Siegel, M.D.

Here's My Credo:

All I really need to know about how to live and what to do and how to be I learned in kindergarten.... These are the things I learned:

Share everything • Play fair • Don't hit people • Put things back where you found them • Clean up your own mess • Don't take things that aren't yours • Say you're sorry when you hurt somebody • Wash your hands before you eat • Flush • Warm cookies and cold milk are good for you • Live a balanced life — learn some and think some and draw and paint and sing and dance and play and work every day some •

Take a nap every afternoon • When you go out into the world, watch out for traffic, hold hands, and stick together • Be aware of wonder • Remember the little seed in the Styrofoam cup: The roots go down and the plant goes up and nobody really knows how or why, but we are all like that • Goldfish and hamsters and white mice and even the little seed in the Styrofoam cup — they all die • So do we • And then remember the Dick-and-Jane books and the first word you learned — the biggest word of all — LOOK • Everything you need to know is in there somewhere •

— Robert Fulghum

Education is one of the great joys and solaces of life. It gives us a framework for understanding the world around us and a way to reach across time and space to touch the thoughts and feelings of others.

But education is more than schooling. It is a cast of mind, a willingness to see the world with an endless sense of curiosity and wonder.

If you would be truly educated, you must adopt this cast of mind. You must open yourself to the richness of your everyday experience — to your own emotions, to the movements of the heavens and the language of birds, to the privations and successes of people in other lands and other times, to the artistry in the hands of the mechanic and the typist and the child. There is no limit to the learning that appears before us. It is enough to fill us each day a thousand times over.

— Kent Nerburn

"When you wake up in the morning, Pooh," said Piglet at last, "what's the first thing you say to yourself?"
"What's for breakfast?" said Pooh.
"What do *you* say, Piglet?"
"I say, I wonder what's going to happen exciting *today*?" said Piglet.
Pooh nodded thoughtfully.

— A. A. Milne

Life is too good to waste a day. It's up to you to make it sweet.

— Sadie Delany

Most of us miss out on life's big prizes. The Pulitzer. The Nobel. Oscars. Tonys. Emmys. But we're all eligible for life's small pleasures. A pat on the back. A kiss behind the ear. A four-pound bass. A full moon. An empty parking space. A crackling fire. A great meal. A glorious sunset.... Don't fret about copping life's grand awards. Enjoy its tiny delights. There are plenty for all of us.

— Anonymous

I once had a professor who dreamed of being a concert pianist. Fearing the possibility of failure, he went into academics where the work was secure and the money predictable. One day, when I was talking to him about my unhappiness in my graduate studies, he walked over and sat down at his piano. He played a beautiful glissando and then, abruptly, stopped. "Do what is in your heart," he said. "I really wanted to be a concert pianist. Now I spend every day wondering how good I might have been."

Find what it is that burns in your heart and do it. Choose a vocation, not a job, and your life will have meaning and your days will have peace.

— Kent Nerburn

There is a voice inside of you
That whispers all day long,
"I feel that this is right for me,
I know that *this* is wrong."
No teacher, preacher, parent, friend
Or wise man can decide
What's right for you — just listen to
The voice that speaks inside.

— Shel Silverstein

We all have all of the answers within us,
if we just listen to ourselves.

— Spencer Johnson, M.D.

If you come to a thing with no preconceived notions of what that thing is, the whole world can be your canvas. Just dream it, and you can make it so. I believe I belong wherever I want to be, in whatever situation or context I place myself.

— Whoopi Goldberg

Life glows with infinite possibilities.

— Anonymous

Be yourself; an original is always better than a copy.

— Anonymous

Remember always that you have not only the right to be an individual, you have an obligation to be one.

— Eleanor Roosevelt

I don't have enough words, but I also want to wish to all of you: Try to find happiness in every day.

— Ekaterina Gordeeva

Here's what I would love to say: "You are rare; you're special, unique, and important. You can make a difference in the lives of other people. Over ten billion people have walked the earth, but there is not now, there never has been, and there never will be another one quite like you. Your voice pattern is different from any other voice on earth; your fingerprints are different; your very genes leave their trail of identifying marks completely different from any human being who has ever lived. You're a special individual. Develop your uniqueness; apply it by using the principles we have been discussing and make a real effort to be a difference maker in other lives."

— Zig Ziglar

Graduation Thoughts to Always Remember... and One Thing to Never Forget

Your presence is a present to the world • You're unique and one of a kind • Your life can be what you want it to be • Take the days just one at a time • Count your blessings, not your troubles • You'll make it through whatever comes along • Within you are so many answers • Understand, have courage, be strong • Don't put limits on yourself • So many dreams are waiting to be realized • Decisions are too important to leave to chance • Reach for your peak, your goal, your prize • Nothing wastes more energy than worrying • The longer one carries a problem, the heavier it gets • Don't take things too seriously • Live a life of serenity, not a life of regrets • Remember that a little love goes a long way • Remember that a lot goes forever • Remember that friendship is a wise investment • Life's treasures are people... together • Realize that it's never too late • Do ordinary things in an extraordinary way • Have health and hope and happiness • Take the time to wish upon a star •

And don't ever forget...
    for even a day... how very special you are.

— Douglas Pagels

Now this is not the end. It is not even the beginning of the end. But it is, perhaps, the end of the beginning.

— Winston Churchill

Let us never be betrayed into saying we have finished our education; because that would mean we had stopped growing. There is always the upward dimension possible for us.

— Julia H. Gulliver

There is a story that contains excellent guidance for those who wonder if they should have more education. The story is about three horsemen of ancient times who were riding across a desert. As they crossed the dry bed of a river, out of the darkness a voice called, "Halt."

They obeyed. They were told to dismount, pick up a handful of pebbles, put the pebbles in their pockets and remount.

After they had done as they were instructed, the voice said, "You have done as I commanded. Tomorrow at sun-up you will be both glad and sorry." The three horsemen rode away thinking about the strange prediction.

The next morning at sunrise, they reached into their pockets and found that a miracle had happened. Instead of pebbles, they pulled out diamonds, rubies, and other precious stones. Then they saw the truth of the prophecy. They were both glad and sorry — glad they had taken some, and sorry they had not taken more....

And this is the story of education.

— Louis O. Caldwell

Often when you think you're at the end of something, you're at the beginning of something else. I've felt that many times. My hope for all of us is that "the miles we go before we sleep" will be filled with all the feelings that come from deep caring — delight, sadness, joy, wisdom — and that in all the endings of our life, we will be able to see the new beginnings.

— Fred Rogers

And by-and-by Christopher Robin came to an end of the things, and was silent, and he sat there looking out over the world...

— A. A. Milne

Looking back at graduation, a young lady recalled "...this is the way it was: a time of joy, then the stirrings of doubt... goodbye to friends, some forever... memory of all the good things, the warm feelings of belonging... search for knowledge revealing frightening new lands... and now... where to now?"

— Louis O. Caldwell

The old... is fast slipping back behind us.
We cannot stay it if we would. We must
go on and leave our past. Let us go forth
nobly. Let us go as those whom greater
thoughts and greater deeds await beyond.

— Phillips Brooks

I hope your thoughts and deeds take you...
to the corners of your smiles,
to the highest of your hopes,
to the windows of
     your opportunities,
and to the
most special places
     your heart
          has ever known.

— Douglas Pagels

Hold on to your dreams, and never let them go • Show the world how wonderful you are • Wish on a star that shines in your sky • Rely on all the strength you have inside • Stay in touch with those who touch your life with love • Look on the bright side and don't let adversity keep you from winning • Be yourself, because you are filled with special qualities that have brought you this far, and that will always see you through • Keep your spirits up • Make your heart happy, and let it reflect on everything you do!

— Douglas Pagels

What Should You Tell the World?

Thou hast seen nothing yet.

— Miguel de Cervantes

Out of the strain of the Doing,
into the peace of the Done.

— Julia Louise Woodruff

I came, I saw, I conquered. [*Veni, vidi, vici.*]

— Julius Caesar

To be what we are, and to become what we are capable of becoming, is the only end of life.

— Robert Louis Stevenson

So be sure when you step.
Step with care and great tact
and remember that Life's
a Great Balancing Act.
And will you succeed?
Yes! You will, indeed!
(98 and $^3/_4$ percent guaranteed.)

— Dr. Seuss

This is the time of endings,
but of new beginnings, too.

Another hope, another chance,
another road to take.
Another star to follow,
and another start to make.

— Anonymous

ACKNOWLEDGMENTS

We gratefully acknowledge the permission granted by the following authors, publishers, and authors' representatives to reprint poems or excerpts from their publications.

HarperCollins Publishers for "I want to be..." from LETTERS FOR ALL OCCASIONS by Alfred Stuart Myers. Copyright 1952 by Barnes & Noble; revised edition copyright © 1993 by HarperCollins Publishers, Inc. All rights reserved. And for "Tell yourself..." from YOUR ERRONEOUS ZONES by Dr. Wayne W. Dyer. Copyright © 1976 by Wayne W. Dyer. All rights reserved. And for "It would be nice..." by Bernie S. Siegel, M.D from AXIOMS FOR SURVIVORS by Lon G. Nungesser. Copyright © 1990, 1992 by Lon G. Nungesser. All rights reserved. And for "There is a voice..." from FALLING UP by Shel Silverstein. Copyright © 1996 by Shel Silverstein. All rights reserved. And for "Remember always..." from YOU LEARN BY LIVING by Eleanor Roosevelt. Copyright © 1960 by Eleanor Roosevelt. Copyright renewed 1988 by Franklin A. Roosevelt. All rights reserved.

Warner Books, Inc., for "Success is feeling good..." from SIMPLE ABUNDANCE by Sarah Ban Breathnach. Copyright © 1995 by Sarah Ban Breathnach. Reprinted by permission of Warner Books, Inc. All rights reserved. And for "I don't have..." from MY SERGEI by Ekaterina Gordeeva. Copyright © 1996 by Ekaterina Gordeeva. Reprinted by permission of Warner Books, Inc. All rights reserved.

Random House Children's Books, a division of Random House, Inc., for "You have brains..." from OH, THE PLACES YOU'LL GO! by Dr. Seuss, TM & copyright © by Dr. Seuss Enterprises, L.P. 1990. All rights reserved.

Ballantine Books, a division of Random House, Inc., for "Along the way..." from DAYS OF GRACE by Arthur Ashe and Arnold Rampersad. Copyright © 1993 by Jeanne Moutoussamy-Ashe and Arnold Rampersad. All rights reserved. And for "When I look..." from STILL ME by Christopher Reeve. Copyright © 1998 by Cambria Productions, Inc. All rights reserved. And for "Here's My Credo" from ALL I REALLY NEED TO KNOW I LEARNED IN KINDERGARTEN by Robert Fulghum. Copyright © 1986, 1988 by Robert L. Fulghum. All rights reserved.

William Morrow and Company, Inc., a division of HarperCollins Publishers, for "I can do anything" and "If you come..." from WHOOPI GOLDBERG BOOK by Whoopi Goldberg. Copyright © 1997 by Whoopi Goldberg. All rights reserved. And for "We all have..." from THE ONE MINUTE SALES PERSON by Spencer Johnson, M.D. and Larry Wilson. Copyright © 1984 by Candle Communications Corporation. All rights reserved.

Ladies' Home Journal for "I'd like to do..." by Barbra Streisand from "Barbra Streisand: Her New Life" by Christopher Nicken (January 1988, p. 38). Copyright © 1988 by Meredith Corporation. All rights reserved. And for "I think the ones..." by Oprah Winfrey from "Oprah Winfrey, Wonder Woman" by Linden Gross (December 1988, p. 40). Copyright © 1988 by Meredith Corporation. All rights reserved.

Curtis Brown, Ltd., for "Indeed, everybody wants...." from KINDLY UNHITCH THAT STAR, BUDDY by Ogden Nash, published by Little, Brown and Company. Copyright © 1935 by Ogden Nash, renewed. All rights reserved.

McGraw-Hill for "There are a lot of..." from WAKE-UP CALLS by Joan Lunden. Copyright © 2001 by New Life Entertainment, Inc. All rights reserved.

Dutton, a division of Penguin Putnam, Inc., for "What matters..." from SO FAR by Kelsey Grammer. Copyright © 1995 by Kelsey Grammer. All rights reserved.

American Association of Retired Persons for "We were privileged..." by Ethel Percy Andrus from THE WISDOM OF ETHEL PERCY ANDRUS. Copyright © 1968 by the National Retired Teachers Association and AARP. All rights reserved.

Hyperion for "Often when you think..." from THE WORLD ACCORDING TO MISTER ROGERS by Fred Rogers. Copyright © 2003 by Fred Rogers. Reprinted by permission. All rights reserved.

New World Library for "Education is one..." and "I once had..." from SIMPLE TRUTHS by Kent Nerburn. Copyright © 1996 by Kent Nerburn. Reprinted by permission of New World Library, www.newworldlibrary.com. All rights reserved.

Dutton Children's Books, a division of Penguin Young Readers Group, a Member of Penguin Group (USA) Inc., 345 Hudson St., New York, NY 10014, for "'When you wake up...,'" from WINNIE-THE-POOH by A. A. Milne, illustrated by E. H. Shepard. Copyright 1926 by E.P. Dutton, renewed 1954 by A. A. Milne. All rights reserved. And for "And by-and-by..." from THE HOUSE AT POOH CORNER by A. A. Milne, Illustrations by E. H. Shepard. Copyright 1928 by E.P. Dutton, renewed © 1956 by A. A. Milne. All rights reserved.

The Gale Group for "Life is too good..." from HAVING OUR SAY: THE DELANY SISTERS' FIRST 100 YEARS by Sarah L. Delany and G.K. Hall. Copyright © 1994 by G.K. Hall. Reprinted by permission of The Gale Group. All rights reserved.

Thomas Nelson, Inc., Nashville, TN, for "Here's what I would..." from ZIGLAR ON SELLING by Zig Ziglar. Copyright © 1991 by Zig Ziglar. All rights reserved.

Baker Books, a division of Baker Book House Company, for "There is a story..." and "Looking back..." from AFTER THE TASSEL IS MOVED by Louis O. Caldwell. Copyright © 1968, 1972 by Baker Book House Company. All rights reserved.

A careful effort has been made to trace the ownership of selections used in this anthology in order to obtain permission to reprint copyrighted material and give proper credit to the copyright owners. If any error or omission has occurred, it is completely inadvertent, and we would like to make corrections in future editions provided that written notification is made to the publisher:

BLUE MOUNTAIN ARTS, INC., P.O. Box 4549, Boulder, Colorado 80306.